FORMULA 1

Teaching and literacy notes

Motorsports: Formula 1 teaching notes and activities by Maureen Gallagher, educational consultant and author. These notes and activities will help you make the most of this book with your child or class.

SPEAKING AND LISTENING

• Find out what the child already knows about Formula 1. What else would they like to find out? Look at the contents list together. Discuss which sections look most interesting.

• Do they have a team that they support, and if so, why do they support them. Do they have a favourite driver and what do they like about them?

• Read the section on 'The Team' and discuss the different roles and how important they are. Which role would the child like to have if they were part of a Fomula 1 team?

• Check that the child understands the following terms from the spread 'Early days of Formula 1'; daredevil, fatal, dominated, revolutionary, aerodynamics and technology. Encourage them to use a dictionary to look them up and discuss their meaning in context. Ask them to make a list of any other words they come across that they don't understand to look up afterwards.

READING

• Ask the child to read the spread 'In the pit lane' then ask them to tell you about it. Ask them the following questions:

1) How many people are in the tyre changing crew?

2) How quick was the fastest-ever pit stop?

3) What does the lollipop man do?

• Check the child knows what a glossary and index are, then ask them to use the glossary to find the meaning of the terms: bhp, debut. Use the index to look up the terms 'slicks' and 'oversteer'

WRITING

• Ask the child to write a list of the safety features that keep drivers safe from serious injury when they crash. They can refresh their memories of what these are by reading page 25.

• Imagine you are a journalist describing a grand prix race and write a newspaper report of the race. Use the template below to help you.

1) Main heading
2) Sub-heading which summarises the main point in a punchy way
3) Picture
4) Who was involved, what happened, where, when
5) Quote from someone who was involved

• Ask the child to write a review of the book. Did it cover all the key points the child expected, was it informative and clear, and were the pictures good. Could it have been improved?

Across the curriculum

MATHS
• Below are the lap times for a four lap race. Work out who has won. What order do they come in?

Driver	Lap 1	Lap 2	Lap 3	Lap 4	Position
Button	2 min 25 sec	3 min 5 sec	2 min 10 sec	3 mins	
Hamilton	2 min 30 sec	1 min 59 sec	2 min 5 sec	2 mins 40 sec	
Webber	1 min 59 sec	2 min 40 sec	1 min 55 sec	2 min 30 sec	
Vettel	2 min 30 sec	1 min 55 sec	2 min 35 sec	2 min 10 sec	

ART
• Design and draw your own Formula 1 car. Use the pictures in the book as a reference to help you.

GEOGRAPHY
• Find out where all the current Formula 1 grand prix races take place and then find each place on a map of the world.

DESIGN AND TECHNOLOGY
• Design your own race track. For inspiration, look up Hermann Tilke on the Internet and check what he says about track design; he is the most famous and successful modern grand prix track designer. Look at the outline of some of the tracks he has designed, such as those in Bahrain and China. You might want to incorporate some of these features into your design.

motorsports

FORMULA 1

Paul Mason

W
FRANKLIN WATTS
LONDON·SYDNEY

This edition 2012

First published in 2009
by Franklin Watts

Copyright © Franklin Watts 2009

Franklin Watts
338 Euston Road
London NW1 3BH

Franklin Watts Australia
Level 17/207 Kent Street
Sydney, NSW 2000

Planning and production by
Tall Tree Limited
Editor: Rob Colson
Designer: Jonathan Vipond

Dewey number 796.72

ISBN 978 1 4451 0727 1

Printed in China

Franklin Watts is a division of Hachette
Children's Books, an Hachette UK company.

www.hachette.co.uk

Picture credits:
BMW AG: 6, 10, 11, 12 bottom, 13, 18 middle, 23, 26, 29 middle left, 29 bottom right.
Corbis: 9 bottom (Schlegelmilch), 16 (Schlegelmilch), 24 bottom (Schlegelmilch), 27 (China Photos/Reuters).
Dreamstime: cover middle (Afby71), cover bottom left (Chris Nolan), cover bottom middle (Afby71), cover bottom right (Shaiful Rizal Mohd Jaafar), 3 (Afby71), 13 middle right (Davejob), 14–15 (Afby71), 15 bottom right (Andrea Presazzi), 29 top left (Afby71).
Getty Images: 7 (AFP), 8 (Hulton Getty collection), 9 top (Popperfoto), 17 middle left (AFP), 17 right, 19, 20–21, 24–25, 29 bottom left, 29 top right.
iStockphoto: 18 top and bottom (ptilley).
Mark McArdle/GNU: 15 top right, 29 right middle
Morio/GNU: 22
Shell Motorsport: 12–13

Every attempt has been made to clear copyright. Should there be any inadvertent omission, please apply to the publisher for rectification.

CONTENTS

THE BIGGEST PRIZE

A man dangles a sign by the side of the track. It reads: "Massa +1.7". Lewis Hamilton's McLaren howls past in a blur, followed a heartbeat later by the red Ferrari of rival Felipe Massa. Blink and you'll miss them.

Welcome to the heat of battle in a Formula One race.

A POPULAR MOTOSPORT

Formula One is the world's most popular motorsport championship. The races – in Europe, Asia, Australia, and North and South America – always attract giant crowds. The Italian fans, or *tifosi*, are especially famous for their **fanatical** support.

△ Felipe Massa, in a Ferrari, leads Lewis Hamilton's McLaren through the first corner of the Turkish **Grand Prix**.

RACING AROUND THE WORLD

Formula One (F1) is motorsport's top motor racing series. F1 races, known as Grand Prix (French for 'big prize'), are held all over the world. Teams and drivers compete against each other in a season that consists of up to 18 Grand Prix. Some races, such as Monaco, take place on closed roads. Most, however, are held on purpose-built race tracks.

A SEASON OF RACING

The Formula One season lasts from spring until late autumn. The drivers and teams are awarded points according to where they finish in each race. At the end of the season, the points are added up to decide the champion driver and team. In 2008, after a nail-biting final race in Brazil, Lewis Hamilton of the UK won the Drivers' Championship, and Italian team Ferrari was the leading team.

▽ British driver Lewis Hamilton celebrates victory in the 2008 Chinese Grand Prix, one of the five races he won on the way to clinching the 2008 Drivers' Championship.

EARLY DAYS OF FORMULA 1

The first Grand Prix drivers were real daredevils. They raced in cars with hardly any safety features and crashes were often fatal. Between 1954–94, 27 Formula One drivers died in crashes. Cars are now much safer and no driver has been killed since 1994.

EARLY MOTOR RACING

Early motor races were held on public roads. Watching was almost as dangerous as driving and many **spectators** were killed in crashes. In the early 1900s, the authorities decided that racing should only be allowed on **closed circuits** and Grand Prix racing was born.

◁ Early races, such as this one in Scotland in 1908, often went right through towns.

THE FANGIO ERA

The first Formula One championship was held in 1950. One driver soon dominated: Juan Manuel Fangio. The Argentine driver won the world championship in 1951 and every year from 1954–57. Fangio's battles with drivers such as Britain's Stirling Moss made Formula One increasingly popular.

△ Juan Manuel Fangio, in car 18, alongside German rival Karl Kling. Both are driving Mercedes cars in the 1954 French Grand Prix.

TECHNICAL DATA

In 1971, Peter Gethin won the Italian Grand Prix with an average speed of 242.616 kph. It was the fastest Grand Prix ever.

THE LOTUS YEARS

During the 1960s, a new power dominated Formula One: the British Lotus team. Lotus used revolutionary materials and **aerodynamics** to gain an edge on other teams. Ever since, **technology** has been crucial to success in Formula One.

▽ By 1969, car design had moved on as Graham Hill's Lotus shows.

THE TEAM

Each team has two racing drivers. They are the ones who will stand on the podium if they come first, second or third. But any driver will admit that winning, or even racing, would be impossible without his team.

DESIGNING A CAR

A Formula One team's **engineers** start work on their new season's car months before the racing begins. Once the racing is underway, they carry on making changes. They constantly **analyse** and modify the car to improve its performance.

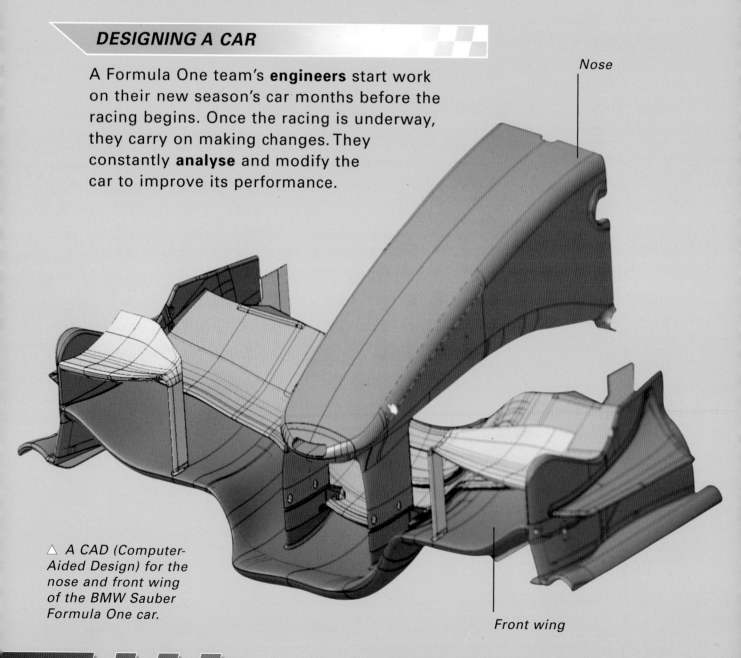

Nose

Front wing

△ A CAD (Computer-Aided Design) for the nose and front wing of the BMW Sauber Formula One car.

TEST DRIVERS

Once a car has been developed, the test drivers get their hands on it. Their job is to drive thousands of kilometres at **race pace**. The information the team gets from this helps to improve the car's speed, handling and **reliability**.

△ Test drivers pass information about the car's performance directly to the team.

MECHANICS

Mechanics travel to each Grand Prix with the drivers. If the car is damaged in practice or during the race, it is their job to repair it. If the driver crashes in practice, the mechanics may have to rebuild the car overnight!

TECHNICAL DATA

Formula One's rules say that no team can do more than 15,000 km of testing in each calendar year. That's far enough to drive nearly halfway round the world.

THE CAR: SPEEDING UP – AND SLOWING DOWN

The top speed of a Formula One car is about 360 kph. How do the cars get up to such high speeds? Just as importantly, how are they able to slow down quickly enough to get round corners?

TECHNICAL DATA

Formula One engines suck in an amazing 450 litres of air a second! They travel just 0.7 km on a litre of fuel.

Rear wing

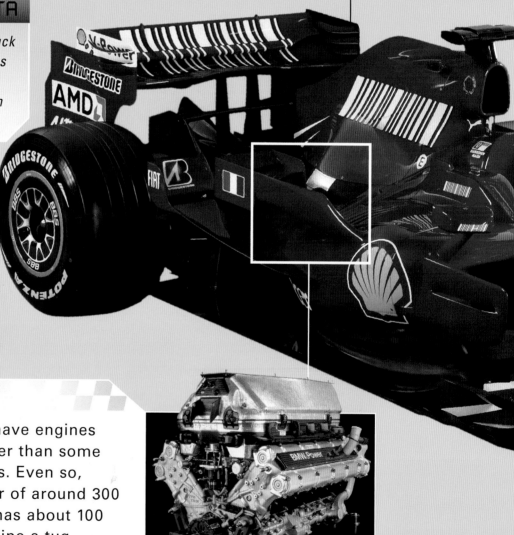

▷ *The Ferrari car driven by Brazilian Felipe Massa.*

GO POWER

Formula One cars have engines of 2.4 litres – smaller than some ordinary family cars. Even so, they produce power of around 300 **bhp**. A normal car has about 100 bhp of power. Imagine a tug of war between the two!

AERODYNAMICS

Aerodynamics describes the way a moving object slips through the air. Formula One cars are designed to be able to slip through the air as easily as possible. This allows them to reach the highest speeds and gives them the best **fuel consumption**.

◁ *A computer simulation shows how air flows over a Formula One car travelling at high speed.*

STOP POWER

Formula One cars stop when two pads grip a brake disc attached to each wheel. Sometimes the cars brake so hard that their discs glow yellow-hot. Brake discs for normal races are made of **carbon fibre**. In wet races, steel discs allow the pads more grip.

Brake disc

Front wing

THE CAR: GRIP

Formula One cars corner at speeds well over 200 kph. That's so fast that the drivers need a special harness to keep them from being thrown out of their seats. How do the cars grip the track so hard?

SUSPENSION

A car's suspension flexes up and down, keeping the tyres in contact with the ground even over bumps and **kerbs**. The suspension also absorbs some of the forces created when a car goes round corners.

▲ The suspension on Vitantonio Liuzzi's Scuderia Toro Rosso car keeps it running smoothly over the kerb.

TECHNICAL DATA

Modern Formula One cars can generate grip that would hold 3.5 times their own weight. In theory, they could be driven upside down!

▷ If drivers take corners too quickly, the rear wheels may not grip the track surface enough and the rear of the car slides out. This is known as oversteer and can cause a car to spin out of control.

AIRFLOW AND GRIP

Changing how air flows over a car affects its grip. On a twisty, slower racetrack, teams set up the airflow to push the car down hard, giving the tyres more grip. On a fast, straight racetrack, they let the air flow smoothly over the car, giving it more speed.

Intermediate tyres

Wet tyres

TYRES

The car's tyres are what hold the car to the track. Teams can choose between dry, wet or intermediate tyres, depending on the weather conditions. Dry tyres, called 'slicks', are smooth. Wet and intermediate tyres are **grooved**.

PRACTICE AND QUALIFYING

Formula One weekends start with a practice session. Next comes qualifying, which can be the most important part of the weekend. Qualifying times decide the drivers' order on the starting grid, where being at the front is a big advantage.

PRACTICE

Every Grand Prix driver's weekend starts with practice. During practice, the drivers get used to the circuit. At the same time, the teams make decisions about the best tyres, suspension and aerodynamics to use in qualifying.

QUALIFYING

During the early qualifying sessions, all the drivers try to record the fastest lap they can. The drivers who set the ten fastest laps get to take part in the final qualifying session.

△ Lewis Hamilton crosses the finishing line during qualifying at Indianapolis, USA.

FINAL QUALIFYING

In final qualifying, the fastest ten drivers have a 'shoot-out' to decide their grid positions for the start of the race. Each tries to set the fastest **flying lap**. Getting a good grid position is especially important on racetracks where overtaking is difficult, such as Hungary and Valencia.

▷ *Qualifying times decide who starts at the front of the grid for the actual race. The best place to start from is known as* ***pole position***.

△ *McLaren's Ron Dennis keeps an eye on the progress of rivals Ferrari during qualifying for the Belgian Grand Prix.*

TECHNICAL DATA

At the 2008 Italian Grand Prix, Sebastian Vettel became the youngest driver ever to be on pole position. At just 21 years old, Vettel then went on to win, making him the youngest-ever winner, too.

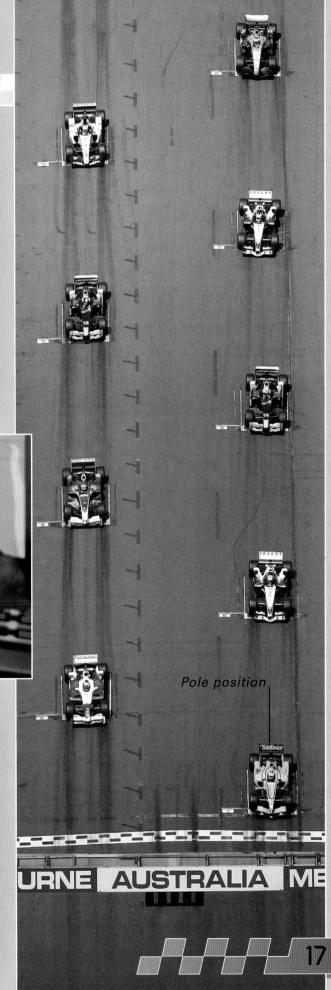

Pole position

AUSTRALIA

THE START

A driver can gain several places on the other racers if he gets off to a good start. Some drivers, such as Felipe Massa and Lewis Hamilton, are famous for fast starts.

SIGHTING LAP

Before the actual start, all the cars do a 'sighting lap'. During the sighting lap the drivers weave across the track, accelerate and brake hard, keeping their cars warmed up for the race.

◁ The green lights come on to signal the start of the sighting lap.

STARTING LIGHTS

After the sighting lap, the drivers line up on the grid. The starting lights begin to come on: one red, then two, three, four, five red lights show. When the lights go out, it's the signal to race away from the line!

▽ All the red start lights light up: when they go out, it's foot to the floor time.

Ready...!

...Get set!

...GO!

△ Three red lights mean it's almost time to go at the Australian Grand Prix.

TECHNICAL DATA

It's not always impossible to win from the back. In the 1983 US Grand Prix, John Watson started 22nd on the grid and finished first.

THE FIRST CORNER

Formula One cars have special 'launch control' systems to help the drivers get a good start. Even so, some drivers always get off faster than others. Everyone wants to reach the first corner ahead of the pack!

△ *Felipe Massa loses control of his Ferrari at the first bend of the Australian Grand Prix. Only the drivers' lightning-quick reflexes prevent mass pile-ups when this happens.*

IN THE PIT LANE

During the race, the drivers have to stop to take on fuel and fresh tyres. This means they have to pull into the pit lane for their pit crew to work on the car. Every member of the pit crew has an important job to do, as even a one or two second delay could cost the team victory.

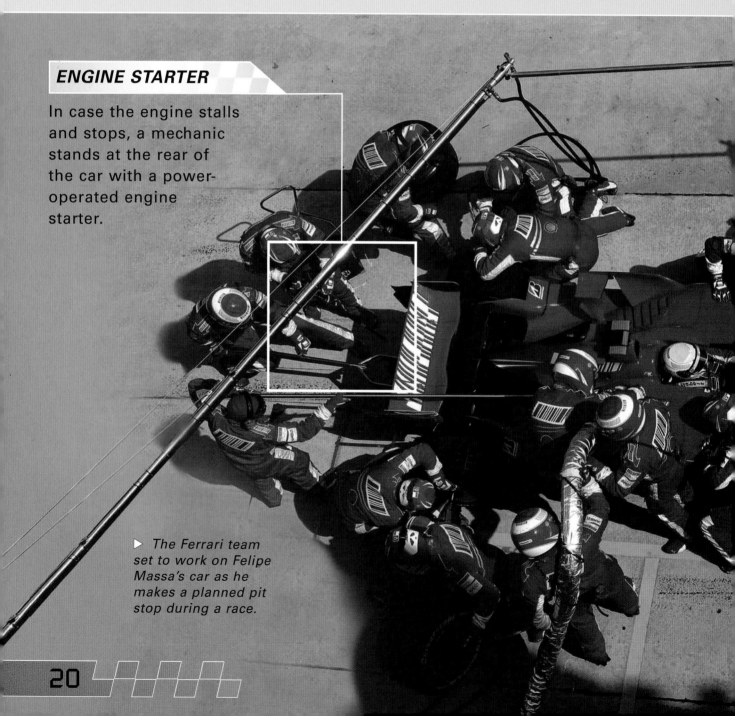

ENGINE STARTER

In case the engine stalls and stops, a mechanic stands at the rear of the car with a power-operated engine starter.

▶ The Ferrari team set to work on Felipe Massa's car as he makes a planned pit stop during a race.

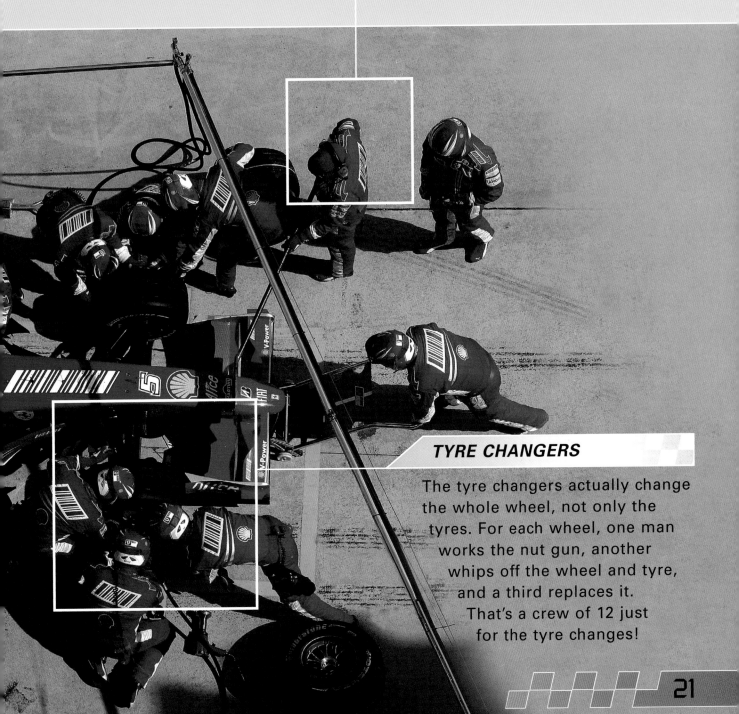

TECHNICAL DATA

The fastest-ever pit stop in Formula One took just 3.2 seconds! It happened in 1993, when Benetton driver Riccardo Patrese was given fresh tyres.

LOLLIPOP MAN

The lollipop man is there to let the driver know what to do. He holds out a sign to keep the driver at a standstill. When the stop is almost over, he turns the lollipop around to warn the driver that he needs to be ready to leave.

TYRE CHANGERS

The tyre changers actually change the whole wheel, not only the tyres. For each wheel, one man works the nut gun, another whips off the wheel and tyre, and a third replaces it. That's a crew of 12 just for the tyre changes!

RACE STRATEGY

Teams can have the fastest car, the best drivers and a brilliant pit crew, but still not win races. The reason is usually that something has gone wrong with their race strategy – the plans they made before the race started.

TYRE CHANGES

Formula One cars have to stop during races to change tyres. Teams can make unlimited pit stops, but usually make two or three. They have to watch out for tyre wear and punctures. Some damage to the car bodywork can be repaired during a pit stop.

▽ *Nico Rosberg in a Williams outbrakes Nick Heidfeld's BMW Sauber to overtake on the inside. There are normally very few places to overtake, so drivers must plan their moves carefully.*

PIT-STOP WINDOWS

Team 'pit-stop windows' are the times in the race when a pit stop must be made. For example, the first window could be between lap 19–21. If a car gets caught behind a slower one on lap 19, it might be a good idea to come in. If the slower car makes its pit stop on lap 19, the driver behind might be able to complete two fast laps before stopping.

△ Robert Kubica comes into the pits to change tyres. Teams must change tyres at least once during the race.

VARYING STRATEGY

There are lots of things that can force a team's strategy to change during the race. For example, a crash might mean an early pit stop is a good idea. Or if it stops raining, the drivers might have to come in for new tyres.

TECHNICAL DATA

While travelling down the pit lane, Formula One cars must not do more than 80 kph. In the tight Monaco pit lane, this is reduced to 60 kph.

RACE SAFETY

With speeds of over 300 kph and drivers dicing with each other just inches apart, Formula One looks like a dangerous sport. It can be, but there are lots of safety measures in place to make it as safe as possible.

TRACK SAFETY

Modern racetracks have lots of safety features. On corners where crashes are likely, there are run-off areas to allow the cars to slow down if they slide off. Gravel traps slow down the cars more quickly. When a crash does happen, marshals wave flags to warn other drivers to take care.

△ *A crane lifts crashed cars out of the gravel at the European Grand Prix in Germany.*

DRIVER SAFETY

If they are unlucky enough to crash, today's drivers have excellent protection:

- They wear fireproof Nomex suits, and a HANS device (which stands for Head And Neck Support) to protect them from serious neck injuries.

- A safety cage stops drivers being crushed in an accident. The sides are made of the same material as bulletproof vests, to stop splinters of metal hitting the driver.

- The outer bodies of Formula One cars are designed to crumple in an accident, absorbing the force of the crash.

△ *The outer body of Robert Kubica's car completely crumpled when he crashed at the Canadian Grand Prix in 2007. The safety cage surrounding his cockpit meant that Kubica escaped unharmed.*

TECHNICAL DATA

Race drivers' Nomex suits would allow them to survive for 11 seconds in temperatures of 840ºC. That's hotter than some volcanic lava!

RACING AROUND THE WORLD

As the Formula One teams travel the world, they visit lots of different kinds of racetrack. Some are old racing circuits layered in history. Others are ultra-modern tracks built in the last few years.

STREET CIRCUITS

Street circuits are racetracks that are also used as public roads (although not while the races are happening!). The most famous street circuit is Monaco. The newest is in Singapore, where the drivers face the added challenge of driving under floodlights!

▽ The difficult Monaco Grand Prix is raced along the streets of Monte Carlo.

◁ The new Shanghai International Circuit hosted the first ever Chinese Grand Prix in 2004.

PURPOSE-BUILT TRACKS

Today, most Formula One races take place on purpose-built tracks. Generally these tracks are the safest. If cars run off the track, they slide safely to a halt instead of crashing into a wall. There are also places for spectators to sit or get something to eat.

THE KING OF TRACK DESIGN

Many of Formula One's newest racetracks have been designed by Hermann Tilke. Tilke has designed racetracks in Malaysia, Bahrain, China and Turkey. As he is also working on at least four more new circuits, Tilke really is the king of track design!

TECHNICAL DATA

GRAND PRIX VENUES, 2012

1 Australian GP	Melbourne
2 Malaysian GP	Kuala Lumpur
3 Chinese GP	Shanghai
4 Bahrain GP	Sakhir
5 Spanish GP	Catalunya
6 Monaco GP	Monte Carlo
7 Canadian GP	Montréal
8 European GP	Valencia
9 British GP	Silverstone
10 German GP	Hockenheim
11 Hungarian GP	Budapest
12 Belgian GP	Spa-Francorchamps
13 Italian GP	Monza
14 Singapore GP	Singapore
15 Japanese GP	Suzuka
16 Korean GP	Yeongam
17 Indian GP	New Delhi
18 Abu Dhabi GP	Yas Marina
19 USA GP	Austin
20 Brazil GP	Sao Paulo

GLOSSARY

aerodynamics
Flow of air over and around an object.

analyse
Arrive at an understanding or explanation for something.

bhp
Short for brake horsepower, a way of measuring how powerful an engine is. The more bhp an engine has, the more powerful it is.

carbon fibre
A strong, wear-resistant material made of thin strands of carbon stuck together with glue.

closed circuits
Racetracks that are open only to race cars and are usually specially designed with driver and spectator safety in mind.

debut
First appearance.

engineers
People who use science and technology to solve mechanical problems.

fanatical
Extremely enthusiastic.

flying lap
Lap in which the car is already going as fast as it possibly can when it crosses the start line.

fuel consumption
Amount of fuel used to cover a set distance. It is usually measured in litres per 100 kilometres (or miles per gallon).

Grand Prix
Formula One race.

grooved
With narrow tracks cut in.

kerbs
Raised sections at the side of a racetrack.

kph
Short for kilometres per hour; a measurement of speed and time taken.

pole position
First place on the starting grid, the position awarded to the fastest qualifier.

race pace
Speed at which a car would be driven during a race.

reliability
A word used to describe something that is dependable, for example, a car that does not breakdown easily.

spectators
The people watching a race.

technology
Use of science for practical purposes, such as making a car go faster.

STAR DRIVERS

LEWIS HAMILTON

Born: 7 January 1985
Nationality: British

In 2007, Hamilton started his career with the best **debut** season ever, finishing second. He went one better in 2008, winning by just one point.

FELIPE MASSA

Born: 25 April 1981
Nationality: Brazilian

In 2008, Massa emerged as Ferrari's lead driver. His battle with Hamilton for the world championship excited race fans everywhere.

ROBERT KUBICA

Born: 7 December 1984
Nationality: Polish

Behind the pack-leading McLarens and Ferraris, BMW Sauber's Kubica looked the best driver of the 2008 season. He won the Canadian Grand Prix.

FERNANDO ALONSO

Born: 27 July 1981
Nationality: Spanish

Alonso was the youngest ever champion when he won aged 24 in 2005. Lewis Hamilton beat this record in 2008, then Sebastian Vettel in 2010.

KIMI RÄIKKÖNEN

Born: 17 October 1979
Nationality: Finnish

Champion in 2007 by a single point. His greatest drive ever was probably winning the Japanese GP from 17th on the grid. Returned to F1 in 2012.

SEBASTIAN VETTEL

Born: 3 July 1987
Nationality: German

Vettel became the youngest ever champion in 2010 at 23 years old. He won again in 2011, becoming the youngest ever double world champion!

WEBSITES

www.formula1.com
The home site of the Formula One organisation, this is an excellent place to keep up with what's going on during the racing season. It also details where each race will be held, including maps of the tracks. There are very good sections on understanding the sport, current teams and drivers, and a Hall of Fame with information about every Formula One world champion.

www.fia.com
The website of the Fédération Internationale de l'Automobile (International Automobile Federation), which regulates most forms of motorsport – including Formula One. The site is a good way to keep up with the current points standings and the racing calendar, but is not as good for background information as the Formula One site.

www.autosport.com
An excellent magazine site for all kinds of motorsport, especially Formula One. Want to know what Lewis Hamilton thinks about the next race, or who's having tyre problems in practice? This is the place to find out. Great for up-to-date news and current interviews.

Please note: every effort has been made by the Publishers to ensure that these websites contain no inappropriate or offensive material. However, because of the nature of the Internet, it is impossible to guarantee that the contents of these sites will not be altered. We strongly advise that Internet access is supervised by a responsible adult.

INDEX